T0147398

REALIGION

THE SCIENCE OF REALITY

MATTHEW WARE

IUNIVERSE, INC.
NEW YORK   BLOOMINGTON

REALIGION
The Science of Reality

Copyright © 2010 by Matthew Ware

All rights reserved. No part of this book may be used or reproduced by any means, graphic, electronic, or mechanical, including photocopying, recording, taping or by any information storage retrieval system without the written permission of the publisher except in the case of brief quotations embodied in critical articles and reviews.

The views expressed in this work are solely those of the author and do not necessarily reflect the views of the publisher, and the publisher hereby disclaims any responsibility for them.

iUniverse books may be ordered through booksellers or by contacting:

iUniverse
1663 Liberty Drive
Bloomington, IN 47403
www.iuniverse.com
1-800-Authors (1-800-288-4677)

Because of the dynamic nature of the Internet, any Web addresses or links contained in this book may have changed since publication and may no longer be valid.

ISBN: 978-1-4502-3211-1 (sc)
ISBN: 978-1-4502-3212-8 (ebk)

Library of Congress Control Number: 2010907683

Printed in the United States of America

iUniverse rev. date: 5/26/2010

CONTENTS

Chapter 1:
Introduction

What is a Science of Reality?

What is real? What is reality? What is not reality? What isn't real? Is reality something that can be studied scientifically? Or is it wholly personal? Can we even question reality without annihilating it? And is reality an intersubjective phenomenon? What role does language play in the construction of reality? Since organized religion has nothing positive to add to reality, what role does religion play currently? What is the future of religion? And what is a self? Who am I in the context of my self-knowledge? What is an empirical ego, and how do I go about getting one? Am I merely the totality of my experience? What role does fantasy play in the construction of an experience of reality, and how is mysticism explained? What is free-will in the causal continuity of the Universe?

How does one define human autonomy? Is it the freedom to act in the world, on the world? What role does human autonomy play in intersubjectivity? And is there really an objective world? What can we know objectively? How does the self-fulfilling prophesy work? And why does the placebo effect work at all? Since magic and hypnosis are not supernatural phenomenon, what motivation should we put on magicians and hypnotists, and how can we use these talents in everyday life? Why are we not all equal, and in what ways are all people the same? Why are children still oppressed, and why even have prisons? Is there really going to be a global culture? What is culture? What is a society? How do we go about self-enculturation? What is understood as mental illness? What role does mental illness play in society? What is a psychochondriac?

What is money, and do we need it? Will self-enculturation replace teachers with some sort of life-guide? What role does technology have on our knowledge and abilities? Can technology replace humans in all fields of activity? Why would anyone want to be famous? Do we need police? Do we need governments? Can civil war be started from the outside? Who is the truly ideal person, or is this an inherent contradiction? How is self-esteem established and maintained? Why is self-esteem important? What role does one's body, thoughts, feelings, intentions and actions contribute to self-knowledge and self-esteem? Do we need countries at all? What is independence?

Can anarchy work as a political stance? What is the myth of the soul? What are the boundaries of the Universe? What is at the edges of space and time? What is death? What remains beyond a person's body after they die? What is attention, and how does it change from object to object? What is consciousness? What is science?

What is freedom in all its implications? What is time? For our starting point, should we presuppose what is real and work directly from our experience of the Universe, or is this begging the question of what is to be real? Should we start with nothingness, and build up a theory of reality from that? Or should we take as our method the scientific attitude? Since God has no role in a Science of Reality, therefore how are we to understand religious concepts, namely the god-concept?

Is every human action motivated by self-interest? Perhaps self-preservation is a stronger instinct? Is humanity defined by survival? How does mass media influence our opinions? Since interest directs our attention, what directs our interest? How are values formed? What is generalized love compared with personal love? Why do we dream, and what do dreams mean? Our everyday actions make up our true, inner being, so how can we shape our habits intentionally to control our development? What is authenticity? What is simultaneousness? Is imagination what makes humans distinctly human? Is language the only purely transcendental phenomenon? Can we control our thoughts, and if so, how and to what degree? When can't we control our thoughts? Are other people our alter-ego in conversation? How does talking shape the brain?

What is the difference between reality and truth? Is transcendence an ideal goal for human growth? Is the purpose of human life to live intentionally? Could there be criminals without laws? What's wrong with drugs? How do I know I'm not dreaming? Is it that in waking life I can withdraw my attention from the world without the world changing? For a starting point we should take real life as it is lived. Nothing should be presupposed at the beginning. Nothing is necessary. Not scientific theories, not even logic. Not even perception. We begin at the beginning, nothing but empty words without symbol or signification. Not even the question mark has meaning anymore. Subject-predicates have no distinction. Nihilism without anything to remove. Family loyalties, friends, work, nothing available to justify our existence. Even our own existence is uncertain. Such is the beginning of our investigation.

The rational-causal structure of the world need not even hold. I would like to take you, the reader, through a series of thought experiments. What we have before us are words, mere words, not the concrete, actual, physical world. So it is with words that we begin. Words. A uniquely human phenomenon. Word manipulation keeps us from animals, and in reading these words we are immersing ourselves in the human linguistic atmosphere to which mere animals have no access.

PART A

Chapter 2:
The Nature of Science

Numbers

Mathematics is like a language in its own right. It has its symbols and grammar and syntax. And it is defined at every point in its development.

Numbers are such that they can be applied, once obtained, to any object in one's environment, memory, imagination or habit. Numbers are contained in imagination or habits. Numbers are contained in the mind too, and mostly on habit of time awareness such that everyone adorns himself or herself with the time in some way, a truly personal and intersubjective phenomenon. Numbers are the first variable that can be set as a variable. Numbers add, multiply, change rate, subtract, divide, and nullify and set limits. They may go on forever, and this is the first sense in which 'forever' occurs. Being is based on possibilities, which are in turn based on math. But since the axioms of math are tautologies or self-referential circular definitions, and follow logic, it is inherently possible to develop in any brain, even an electronic one. Numbers, like words, hold our awareness and we use that held attention to find an answer to an objective question. Since numbers can have this objective and ever-presentable nature, they can become the basis of comparison, even acting as money or credit. They put magnitudes on things. It is a statistical fact that given a large enough sample size, any pattern intended, even if by emotionally triggered obsession, can become observed. Patterns are observed with the mind, but that does not mean they occur only in the mind. Patterns of nature can become observed.

There are different types of numbers. First there are integers, then real numbers, then complex numbers, then there are vectors that are a length and a direction. This presupposes a frame of reference, whether Cartesian rectangles, polar coordinates meaning circles with angles and length of radius, cylindrical coordinates, and so forth. Numbers can be infinitely divided then added together, called integration, or their rate of change can change, where derivatives come into play. The interesting thing about numbers is that they can be applied to anything perceivable, either dividing a thing into smaller parts or by grouping things into a larger whole by adding them.

Every quantitative science makes use of numbers. The value of arbitrary constants is based on standards set by agencies around the world, like the kilogram, the meter and the second. Agreed upon mutual use makes standards of measurement possible, one way in which science is a social phenomenon. What significance numbers have for the Science of Reality has yet to be determined.

THE NULL HYPOTHESIS

Null hypothesis accompanies every experimental question. Basically it is the hypothesis that says nothing happens, that there is no cause-effect relationship. It is equal to zero in mathematics or one in probability, or rather in the sense of certainty of randomness. The null hypothesis states that the observed effect is within the error bounds of the result if based on pure chance alone.

Every experiment makes use of the null hypothesis when making observations. The fact that it is so widely used and is of so little concern is important. The theory of the ether, a substance thought to fill the Universe, was disproved by using the null hypothesis. This experiment thought that light should travel at a different speed if moving with the ether rather than perpendicular to the motion. Since no difference was observed, the null hypothesis took effect and the speed of light was kept constant while all change took place relative to the speed of light. The null hypothesis must be present in every experiment done in the Science of Reality.

THE SELF-FULFILLING PROPHECY

Self-fulfilling prophecy is a temporal gap between a meaningful intention for something to happen and recognition of that intention upon fulfillment. This occurs in the context of many layers of meaningful being sequentially spaced out over time.

The self-fulfilling prophecy is why it is important to be responsible about your beliefs. What you believe can be brought about without your conscious intervention or will-power. If you can change or reframe your beliefs, you can change their influence on your life, thereby changing your life. On the other hand, some things will never exist on the basis of belief alone, no matter how much you believe in it. In the Universe, some things simply cannot exist, some things are mere ideals.

We should use the self-fulfilling prophecy to achieve the important results in our life. We do this by believing with certainty that what we want is going to happen. It is a matter of faith in oneself to bring about the results one wants. If you have to believe in something you should believe in yourself.

THE PLACEBO EFFECT

Placebo effect is an active effect in that something physical is given along with a belief about change. It is this belief that is the active component. Placebo effective treatment should be given as a first resort for non-critical illness and as a last resort for the terminally ill. It is through the placebo effect that homeopathic medicine works, by providing a physical yet inert material around which physical change can take place.

The placebo effect makes use of the self-fulfilling prophecy, but with an added component, namely something physical that holds the place of the placebo. Placebos should have added benefit on children due to their susceptibility to belief and the effects of these beliefs, but only in cases where change of mood would have deeper effects on the course of a non-serious illness.

Anything can serve as a placebo, as long as the belief is accompanied by the placebo. Every drug tested uses a placebo as a control substance, and nearly every placebo has some beneficial effect, though perhaps not as effective as the substance being tested.

A person can create his or her own placebos. This is the only positive effect that religion has, that is, by providing a placebo in the form of a symbol with the belief that your wishes will be fulfilled by some magical power beyond one's control. But that power is within your control. What they do not understand is that this greatest power for change is an inherent power of the human mind.

Psychosomatic Illness

Psychochondriac is defined by being a person who brings about mental illness by thinking about it. Psychosomatic illness is probably the most common illness. By believing one has an illness, it brings attention to the symptoms of the illness and becomes a self-fulfilling prophecy whereby the mind makes possible the infectious illness to enter one's life. By dwelling on the symptoms of an illness, rather than deal with each symptom in isolation, one can bring illness upon oneself, if not physical. Stress is the most common cause of psychosomatic illness.

Even illnesses that are not purely psychosomatic can benefit from positive belief. Wellness can be a self-fulfilling prophecy, and a self-sustaining philosophy on life. As can illness. If you have to believe in yourself, believe you can heal and recover. Believe nothing can stop you from working on recovery.

For those illnesses that are caused by the mind, working out personal problems can give you more energy by freeing your concentration, and can give you a new sense of desire for life. Physical illness can follow relationship problems, death of a loved one, personal setbacks, financial hardship, and basically anything that causes great stress. The Science of Reality may shed light on cures for psychosomatic illness.

Chapter 3:
The Self-Concept

Concepts

The attitudes you hold towards objects determines the relation those objects have to you. Concepts occur as consciousness of something. Concepts have meanings and can be applied over perceptions.

Concepts are not contained in the mind, they are the mind. You can change your concepts by changing your mind.

Concepts make up the model of the world to which we respond. Concepts close off the rest of the world and isolate phenomenon in order to give them an identity.

Concepts have properties, which link them together. One chain of concepts may provide a rational proof while another chain may lead to deception, delusion and hallucination. Logic follows the first while errors in logic lead to the other. However, human beings are not wholly rational beings, and logic is not necessarily a human universal. We are all prone to error and mental illness. Logic is a method, not a cure.

Concepts are immediate, they come into our minds automatically, and they need not refer to anything particular. Language plays a huge role in the construction of concepts. Language allows for finer discriminations to take place and can put labels on concepts so that they may have an independent identity. Concepts are a part of reality, and are therefore necessary for a Science of Reality.

THE SELF

Your attitude towards things prioritizes those things in your life, making up your life from your free intentions. This process categorizes your life and gives it order in a world of chaos.

Self is the ground of all being, yet there is no core that can be called a self since the self is in process of becoming. The self is both the one side of experience and the body that undergoes change. Objects and other people make up the other side of experience and they cannot be separated from the subjective side of conscious experience.

The self is the frame of reference for the ego or self-concept or identity, and also the reference towards objects to which meaning is given by a field of experience. This field is language internalized plus the various submodalities that make up senses, such as pitch, distance, sour, hard, and repugnant in the cases of sound, sight, taste, bodily feeling, smell, all expressed and interpreted through the pathway of language and experience.

The ego or self-concept or identity one accepts as one's own may not be an objective evaluation but more like a journey of self-discovery. Or one can be rigid and dogmatic about their ego and get very aggressive or defensive, effectively breaking off communication. In this way the ego is temporal and social.

Or, one can be too open to feedback from others about themselves. They could take on or reflect the personality, behaviours, tones, slang, and intensity of their conversational participant, never truly reaching a genuine opinion of their own. In fact, there are many attitudes one can take towards oneself, and they may change as time passes, sometimes very rapidly, but it is the present mood and the object of attention that makes up the present, conscious self. The self is the essential starting point in the Science of Reality.

LIMITS OF THE SELF

Limits of the self involve issues of control. What and who can a person control, and what is beyond their personal grasp? Limits of the self also include issues of freedom. What can I do and what can I predict and control? This is the role of science, prediction and control, thereby expanding human ability, even the ability to prolong life.

One limit, one boundary, is the skin. Skin is the outermost organ that is an outreach of you. You have nerves and blood vessels and hair in your skin, and it is continually shedding and rejuvenating. Your skin is alive and a part of you. And it is basically the limit within which you have to control yourself. Without thinking, your body operates automatically, regulating breathing, heart rate, blood sugar level and blood pressure, and so forth, leaving it up to your brain to reveal your surroundings.

The fact that you are alive limits you in some way. It is a fact of life to have a beginning and an end in time, to have a single space-time continuity throughout this the whole span of your life. Also, you may be able to create human life, but remember that this is a new, independent life force that is completely helpless for only the first few months of his or her life.

Death is at the other end of the spectrum. Everything alive dies. The whole dissolves into parts. Upon decomposition of the individual, the body is void of experience, is left forever from family life. There is simply no experience after death. Death is the final limit of the self. An understanding of the process of dying could bring comfort to many.

MULTIPLICITY OF BEING

Multiplicity of being means that each of us is many things simultaneously and that sometimes an object has many uses. It is for this reason that multiple perspectives can be taken towards an object, event or process by the same person or by multiple people at the same time.

Every effect has multiple causes in the cause-effect chain of the Universe. Every interpretation has multiple possibilities from the perspective of the observer.

Being is not singular and isolated but occurs in levels of importance for the moment. This is where values come in, to tell us which levels are most important to pay attention to at the moment. Values direct attention.

Even a person is many things for many people, and hence there is even multiplicity of being inherent in every human being, especially in regard to the social roles we have to play.

Nothing is wholly good or bad but interpretation makes it so. Rather than assign a singular level to something, we should first seek alternative uses for such a thing.

Every event has multiple causes, but in order to study it in isolation, we must look only at the necessary causes, since most causes are mere contingency and therefore not important.

How values draw attention to things in the Universe, and influences our free-will and ability to change the Universe, a Science of Reality needs to study values within a multiplicity of being.

CHAPTER 4:
THE UNIVERSE

LIFE

Life is a self-perpetuating process. Life includes all things in the process of living that is based on DNA, though there are things that have DNA and are not necessarily alive. DNA provides our genetic identity. Plants, animals, insects, etc., are alive, and life is all things living at a specific time since the beginning of the Universe and also since the beginning of life to solar extinction. Life is an open system and needs a source of energy to survive, like our sun. All that is not part of a living system is called inorganic. Living and non-living systems, like oxygen-exchange and transformation systems like photosynthesis, go together to make up an ecosystem. Some species within that ecosystem are reproducible.

All living things are cellular, even single celled organisms. These cells make up all the tissue of the body. A stem cell is a special type of cell that can become whatever type of tissue is nearby. Stem cells may someday provide a cure for cancer, and the cells themselves are harvested before they become any part of an independent organism, or living fetus.

The process of life and the composition of ecosystems has become almost entirely within human grasp and influence. Humanity is a force which challenges natural selection, and environmental control has been accomplished within home, school, factory, store, and car, and may even extend into controlling the weather someday. Ecosystems contain elements of a Science of Reality.

NATURE

Nature consists of all organic and inorganic matter that supports life. Very much like the Universe as a whole, there are laws that perpetuate throughout the whole of nature. Nature as a whole contains ecosystems as well as all that is natural, including human nature. Science is approaching the study of subjective experience, and has already conquered nature, and the Science of Reality would bring more control over an individual's life.

Every organism in nature is unique and human beings are no different. I think that part of what makes human nature unique is our capacity for self-directed learning. Self-directed learning is a life-long process of growth, so although we never grow up, we do continue to grow. This, I believe, is what makes humans unique animals, and makes culture possible.

Nature entails growth, but it also entails death. Death is part of the natural process. New life comes about by the recycling of dead bodies as part of the food chain. Our bodies will be decomposed and eaten by bugs. Nothing can prevent death from naturally occurring. The fact that death occurs need not be frightening. The fact that what we identify with as ourselves, our subjective experience, ends abruptly, without any lingering observer, need not invoke fear. Pain is more frightening than death, and without death, pain is just another feeling.

FUNDAMENTAL LAWS

Fundamental laws persist across all of nature and the whole Universe. They are regularities that persist over all time. Even if only self-fulfilling self-similarities, fundamental laws serve as an approximation or statistical pattern applied to a collection or group.

Fundamental laws need to be continually tested and integrated to make sure we have the right ones. If fundamental laws never change, they should hold up to constant testing. Through a Science of Reality we could conduct these tests.

Rationality, not emotional reasoning, sets up the fundamental laws. Feelings are more the realm of politics, not science, but this is beginning to change. If fundamental laws of human nature could be found, we would have the key to motivate people into action. One such motivation could be the motive to learn the fundamental laws of the Universe, or of nature, or of human nature. Freedom provides a difficulty for understanding the fundamental laws of human nature, as it must be included as part of human nature.

If fundamental laws, like gravity, are found to exist for human nature, we could use them to make inferences about other fundamental laws as well as predictions about the Universe. Very little science is done deductively, but once the fundamental laws have been deduced further inferences about nature can be made.

CONSERVATION AND CAUSALITY

Conservation and causality keep the mass-energy state at a constant. It is one of the assumed foundations of theoretical physics, even to some degree at a quantum level. But what if the fundamental laws of conservation of energy or causal continuity did not in fact apply to the whole Universe always?

Where does freedom enter the chain or field of Universal causality? Is human freedom a black hole in Universal causality? Or can free-will be explained as a fundamental rule of nature?

We enter the actuality of the Universe through a realm of possibilities. Fact is the Universe, experience an actualization of possibilities. From our possibilities we act. Using free-will to choose from possible futures, we act, thereby making an application of mental processes to shape our environment to bring about the results of our intentions. From this we develop a structured past upon which we can reflect and work in imagination to create more future possibilities. Imagination exercises free-will by working out possibilities for consciousness, fine-tuning our ability to direct and focus our conscious attention, and taking on alternate identities to see in imagination what could become actual, and how. The ability to plan requires imagination and flexibility, as well as wisdom, knowledge, and foresight. From all this we act, out of habit or conscious intention. The Science of Reality focuses on how our actions can change the Universe and other minds.

Limits of the Universe

Limits of the Universe include the beginning of space and time, and include the edge of the Universe to the present time, since the start of time, times that many light-years doubled since it expands in two directions away from a center. Perhaps the space-time-energy-matter system reached, or will reach, a threshold of expansion and form an infinitely narrow and wide disk expanding forever in space and time increasing in these proportions infinitely, or rather keeping the volume of the universe steady and never reaching an end space or time that never experienced energy. Could such a place even possibly be said to exist ever?

The speed of light is the upper limit for any velocity, and although an object can accelerate forever, it can never reach the speed of light because space and time fundamentally change at these speeds. The curvature of space-time around mass ensures that light cannot travel fast enough to escape the pull of a black hole. Space or length of time can only be known to a minimum value, though in imagination can be divided infinitely. A star's lifetime is wholly dependent on its mass and composition. The Earth itself will someday be destroyed or cease to support life. Life had a beginning and will have its extinction when the last living being dies. Yet the Universe is what is actual, is the sum total of all that exists, has existed, and will ever exist. Certain myths just aren't real, such as that there is an outside of the Universe beyond space and time, or the existence of supernatural forces or beings.

Chapter 5:
Intersubjectivity

Society and Culture

Society is a collection of people. Culture is meanings embodied in artifacts put to some human use. Society is coherent in that it adapts a specific culture.

Society cannot be separated from culture, nor culture from a specific society. Whether an idea is shared by many people, or one person has many ideas, the two are all but inseparable. However, to subject regard for one multiplies the other, and the same happens if we reverse our regard.

The status-quo is an element of culture subjected to a majority in society. Social norms are the same. Social expectations make up social norms, at least in principle, and to the extent that these roles are fulfilled, one can be said to be a contributing member of society.

Who controls cultural expression? We all do, consciously or otherwise. Everything we think, say and do can be considered a cultural expression, if so interpreted. The age of majority is just another way of disallowing children their inherent freedom to contribute to cultural development of which they are, or should be, an important part with an autonomous voice all their own. They should be allowed to participate in society for its development and constitution. Whereas sociology studies societies, and anthropology studies culture, the Science of Reality finds these two fields inseparable.

MULTIPLE PERSPECTIVES

Multiple perspectives are ways of perceiving an object from multiple points of view. Other people inherently have multiple perspectives on a situation, and in order for it to be the same object for others, many people must be simultaneously conscious of the same object, adding meaning to the object from different sides or multiple angles or perspectives.

Multiple perspectives are useful for objectivity and confirmation of reality. However, there are many people who are similarly deluded and their multiple perspectives just increases the confusion under which such lies can propagate. Mass hysteria, much like mass conformity, underlay many social problems like the stock market crash or war. The ability for a mass of people to share a single perspective underlies all leadership ability and can hold the attention of generations. To stir up such passion for an ideal takes great skill, and is not necessarily a good thing, despite good intentions.

Having the same object take on multiple meanings is why having multiple perspectives can be a good thing. Different angles can be addressed in different ways, and the big picture can be held in mind simultaneously with the details. Empathy requires that a single person can take on other people's perspectives and look for multiple ways to solve another's problems. Multiple perspectives are an inherent part of a Science of Reality.

MEANINGS

Meanings have two sides, the intended side and the fulfilled side. These two sides constitute the meaning of meaning, by fulfilling the questioning attitude.

Meanings are always either meant by someone or interpreted by someone as meaning something. This indicates a temporal and serial succession of one by the other, the intention towards fulfillment. In order for communication to occur, an intention to communicate must be initiated, followed by this recognition. Without this recognition, one feels uncomfortable and follows one awkward comment after another until some form of acknowledgement of pure existence occurs.

Meanings can be related in many ways. One way is common property, another the if/then statement, another with and, and another with another and so on...

Meanings that follow other meanings connected logically or rationally are only a small subset of all possible meaning intention-fulfillments. Mathematics yet another subset. Anything you can become conscious of has meaning for you. It means something for some intention to be fulfilled. Meaning can have layers, due to the multiplicity of being, with words at one level and deeper enrichment following continuously with the context.

Emotions invest meaning with personal value. Therefore, a study of how emotions invest value in objects and other people, as well as one's self, would be invaluable to a Science of Reality.

CONVERSATION

Conversations go back and forth between people, or in circles or cycles around a group or subgroup. Conversations are primarily how people enter into the linguistic atmosphere.

Some people control the linguistic atmosphere with strong emotions, others by telling elaborate stories including all listeners within the plot or focusing all on one. Others are masters of gossip. One way or another we all express ourselves, even by the act of listening. Without this mutual simultaneous engagement over time, one could never tell a story or assign responsibility. One could not manipulate or control. There would be no respect.

By reciprocating type comment with type, it must be obvious what the relationship is between each exchange, because there is an implicit trust not to make it personal, or to make it intimately personal, or somewhere in between. Depth of detail, personal relevance, and contextual relativism all contribute to making exchanges fluid and spontaneous. Moving through the steps of the relationship too fast at these levels can generate mistrust. The self, since self-interest is a universal human motive, probably should ask itself when around others, what are they getting besides my friendship? Usually there's something. But there may not be. Friendship can become a self-fulfilling prophecy with its own rewards. And the way we connect with friends is between mutual conversation, or empathetic shared control of the linguistic atmosphere.

MONEY

Money is a system of social relations based on use-value of the thing or service exchanged for an equivalent of your money that you had to work for. In this way social structures of production and exchange aim mainly as social controls, enforced by a government that authorizes some people, actually allows them the violence that could lead up to murder, namely police reinforcement of the current economic system. Money is not a necessary element of human exchange, and therefore its usefulness should be called into question by a Science of Reality.

Chapter 6:
The Self-Concept and
the Universe

Being a Body

Being a body is quite common. Everyone who exists has a body, but not every body is at this time alive and conscious. Being a body means being a part of the Universe, and a spatial-temporal continuity that changes with each breath. Being a body means having parts that function autonomously but also interconnected into a whole that is 'your body'.

The environment, body, and brain are an organic information-experience-integrator and works as an integrated world.

The human brain is the most complicated element in existence. Its evolution and control of its body shapes its environment to fit its further development. The human brain is the control center of all culture, and the brain is the source of human freedom, by creating possibilities prior to required action and the ability to experience past the moment into the future through expectation.

Having a brain also means having a working body as an extension into the environment. Each body is part of a spatial continuity on both sides, a continuity of space that extends across the whole Universe. You take this space wherever you go, here you are. If you live your body, you are at home anywhere you may find yourself. The body incarnates the genesis of reality.

THIRD-PERSON PERSPECTIVE

Third-person perspective is uniquely human. It means building a model of the world and responding and interacting with that model. Third-person perspective is a model of the Universe without people, or with people as objects in a world or context.

One can work on one's imagination by exercise of the third-person perspective. However, if one spends too long in the third-person perspective they may lose touch with their body or other people.

Using the third-person perspective in imagination helps to understand the rules and regularities of nature and the Universe. Non-fiction literature makes extensive use of the third-person perspective. It takes time to effectively, realistically establish a third-person perspective. Scientists spend years developing this perspective in their minds.

The use of the third-person perspective helps people gain a new point of view on their situation, one devoid of internal feelings, one shaped by the imagination where things are given wholly and completely, instantly, and without mediation of the senses. Out of body experience occurs when the mind disconnects from the senses and enters a realm of pure imagination. The third-person perspective allows us to understand maps and navigation, and our place in the Universe.

Another interpretation of the third-person perspective comes from being the third person in a linguistic environment, where two strangers with knowledge or opinions about you carry on a conversation using you as the referent while keeping their prior conversation the context of remarks or feedback about yourself. The third-person perspective on yourself allows for purely objective feedback about your reputation with others, something that cannot be obtained objectively in the first-person or second-person perspectives. The Science of Reality includes, but is not restricted to, the third-person perspective.

CHAPTER 7:
THE UNIVERSE AND
INTERSUBJECTIVITY

BEING OF OTHERS

Being of others has confused philosophers for centuries. How can we prove others exist, let alone ourselves? But by assuming the being of others as given we are allowing others into our lives as others who are like us. Others also contribute multiple perspectives to a situation.

We are born into a world of others, and initially depend on others for our survival. The being of others naturally imposes expectations on us by others. Being a member of a family places one in a social role. Norms and values initially come from the being of others, and even the rejection of value systems requires others to rebel against them.

All education is a product of the work of others. We assimilate it through enculturation, and later repeat it to others, thereby spreading culture. Culture is inherent in the being of others and requires the being of others to transform and communicate the meanings of cultural objects and their use.

Feelings can be evoked by the being of others, and socializing with others gives you practice expressing, and learning how to react and respond to feelings as they arise, using the insight of other people's experience. To create the attitude of a Science of Reality requires the mass reproduction and creation of its symbolic artifacts, its books and concepts, and all similar works.

BODIES OF OTHERS

Bodies of others gives us the first glimpse into their world, through body language, and allows us to assume that since we each have a body and they have a similar body, they must be like us.

When two bodies come together intimately it is to be together, and in the process, a third body may emerge over time.

Physical contact with another person develops a physical relationship, good or bad. Connecting on the skin makes a single event in space over time, however brief. Physical contact with another body can also be meant as a form of intended harm, and it is usually this intent that hurts more than the pain, at least emotionally.

Other bodies also embody a sense of humanity within oneself. Being a part of the human species provides a sense of comfort and conformity, and fosters good intentions. No matter how depressed we get, we can look to other bodies for recognition that we are not alone and isolated, however much we feel that we are alone in our sorrows.

And being away from the bodies of others may empower us with a sense of freedom since there is no one to stand in our way. However, we may end up lacking the support that other bodies provide. And other bodies can adorn themselves with cultural artifacts, such as the Automat, thereby becoming possible objects of observation.

THE PSYCHOLOGY OF PHYSICISTS

Psychology of physicists presents us with a unique problem. Physics is a branch of science concerned with prediction and control, and hence some physicists apply this attitude to other people. Physics is a closed set of symbolic meanings, and this close mindedness combined with prediction and control sets up a unique problem for physicists interacting with others from outside this worldview.

Physics is also intellectually challenging since it deals mainly in numbers and the third-person perspective. Because of this, no matter how good the intentions, some physicists lose their inherent sense of empathy and their ability to see things from another person's point of view. This is not a necessary consequence, simply a regularity that may occur due to the stresses of the job. Human beings may have evolved to use simple numbers, but control over one's imagination for such long time periods can create great internal stress, if not properly enculturated. And the external demands placed on a physicist, the demanded certainty, and the time pressures make it a requirement to study and train oneself into this role, for the nature of scientific knowledge is continuous, and requires continuous adaptability to identify and address culturally relevant problems. The Science of Reality aims at being such a stable structure of the social consciousness, of culture.

CHAPTER 8:
THE SELF-CONCEPT AND INTERSUBJECTIVITY

EMPATHY

Empathy is another problem faced by philosophy. Empathy is how people connect and share feelings. Empathy is the stance taken towards others and treating others how you would act if you were in their situation.

Empathy requires the second-person perspective. Your emotional style resonates between two people or one person and a group. By taking on the mood of a group and focusing or amplifying it, a leader emerges.

By taking on another's emotional expressions, you have an instant connection to their mind in a very intimate way. It is due to the fact that human beings share a common emotional basis set that makes empathy possible. With empathy, you take on their perspective and worldview, then return to your own experiential resources to help them out of problems.

It requires a great deal of introspection and awareness of one's own emotional state to be able to respond appropriately to someone else's emotions. It also takes practice. But the ability to be triggered into an emotional state by another person's emotional state is an inherent part of human nature and relationships. And the ways these relationships develop usually occurs through conversation, and taking turns manipulating the linguistic atmosphere. We build and share our identities through conversation.

THE SECOND-PERSON PERSPECTIVE

Second person perspective is a way of viewing yourself from someone else's point of view. It allows you to be objective with yourself and opens doorways to other minds. Aside from empathy, sympathy for others also arises from the second-person perspective.

If the intention to communicate precedes or accompanies each communication, the attitude that makes up the intention to communicate gives away many layers of assumptions with each gesture, one such possible interpretation to be the meaning or value you attribute to the person about you in their finite hierarchy of friends, relatives, acquaintances, and strangers with which they have had an interaction.

Empathy is to go through the emotional process of another person, sympathy is sharing only the feeling of remorse or displaced regret.

One problem that occurs when trying to view yourself from two simultaneous viewpoints is that it may cause conflict. From a first-hand perspective, you get experiential access immediately. From a third-hand perspective you imagine or live your body, including your senses as a frame of reference, as part of the environment. Like introspection of the first-hand perspective, imagination also plays a part in the third-hand perspective. And rather than the continuous time of the first, the third is continuous in space, but the second-hand perspective is necessarily inter-social. But how can you accurately think about what is in another's mind, when such thoughts originate from your own mind?

When in conversation with someone, that second person can send mixed messages about what they think about you by the framing of the content of their contribution to the conversation. The third-person perspective occurs in another way, when you walk by a couple in conversation and hear a small sample of the rhythm as they carry on a small conversation about your properties while discussing another topic. All three provide feedback for your self-concept, and thereby to the Science of Reality.

BEING FOR OTHERS

Being for others is a way of being in the world. Being for others allows you to help others with their projects, or, on the other hand, if you want to be a problem for others you could intentionally interfere with or take over their projects for them.

Care is the defining characteristic with which we interact with others. Care for ourselves is one way of being for others, for we can care about what others think of us. But more fundamentally, care for others engages their sense of the world. Taking care of someone else means fulfilling their needs, not necessarily before your own

35

needs because you cannot take care of anther person until you have developed care for yourself, but still entering their model of the world to find out and fulfill the needs of another. This is evident in the early stages of the parent-child relationship.

In pure being for others, you give up your rights and needs and displace them onto another. You treat another how they want to be treated. You become a useful object for them, or otherwise a friend. Friendship is another term for being for others embodied in another person. The helping profession takes on being for others as a business investment, and the primarily tool they use is empathetic shared control of the linguistic atmosphere. They know the right questions to ask, and how and when to ask them. Human service professionals use scientific knowledge and apply it to specific human lives to make change. Hopefully, the Science of Reality can help others in these helping professions.

OTHER MINDS

Other minds are necessary for us, otherwise they would be our minds. By stating that other minds are for us, I also mean they are against us, in the sense that other minds can take on our projects or interfere with them intentionally.

Other minds are a necessary part of human nature, if for no other reason than to develop our own. Our own mind can be other for another but never for ourselves. We have an intimate connection with our own mind in a way that we can never have with other minds. Although we can never have direct access with other minds, we can share a linguistic atmosphere with them, thereby connecting them by focusing attention commonly held to the same object or person. In this way other minds make up a community for us, and provide us with common cultural artifacts like numbers, the alphabet, words, and television shows, among other things. These things were created with the intention of being put to use by other minds, and other minds are the primary source of culture for us, as well as stimulants and objects on which emotions project values. Being human implies a human community of other minds, each at various stages of development.

We are not isolated subjects of pure experience but rely on other minds to help guide us through our actions as we go about our day. However, just because a belief lies in another mind does not necessarily make it true. In fact, other minds present themselves as the limit, the one perspective we can never take in that they also have a body of their own, and situations, like perspectives, change over time.

SELFISHNESS AND SELF-INTEREST

Selfishness and self-interest are humanity's primary motive and goal, to become self-perpetuating and self-supporting, emotionally, socially, introspectively, and so on in all realms of the self. Everybody is born self-interested and there is nothing wrong with standing up for yourself and asserting you inherent right to exist.

Sometimes it's very important to take time for oneself and do something enjoyable. For example, it's O.K. to be selfish with yourself during times of illness in order to allow yourself to get well. It's important to be self-interested during illness and recovery, if nothing else, to make sure you are in fact getting more well rather than worse. If you are getting worse, you should probably do something else about it because it may get worse from there and it takes patience and courage to ask for help when you need it. During this time, try to help yourself, perhaps with self-help books as issues arise and whether ill or not, try to always better yourself. Think of wellness as a process that takes place, in you. You just have to keep changing what you do until you find something that works, use it, and get well again. Then repeat as issues arise. In this way you develop yourself into anything you want to be. Self-interest is one of the fundamental axioms of free-will, and therefore a basic premise of the Science of Reality.

IDENTITY

Identity is the set of beliefs that we take ownership of, and gives us a sense of ourselves. Identities change over time, and there is no absolute core that makes up who we are, aside from the self-coherence of our physical bodies continuously through space and time, and the continuous reflectability of our experience. We also take on the identities of others, something actors are extremely talented at doing.

We are our own rights to sole use. We are in relation to other people, children, parents, any social role or responsibility we take on as our own. We are our bodies, we are our minds and subjective experience, as well as concepts in other people's minds and those relationships. We are many things to many people, even strangers, and have an implicit multiplicity of being.

What is important is who one is to oneself, one's relationship with oneself. One can take a first, second, or third-person perspective with oneself, gaining new information about oneself from each stance.

The self-concept is one's identity to oneself. This includes one's level of self-esteem, made up of their self-respect and self-confidence. Lacking these results in a poor or negative self-image, which may lead to further problems in one's life, making ongoing problems worse, or become a self-fulfilling prophecy of shame and irritation. The Science of Reality hopes to address these issues and solve these problems with a focus on wellness as a self-fulfilling lifestyle.

CHAPTER 9:
RELIGION AND THE NATURE
OF LANGUAGE

THE LINGUISTIC ATMOSPHERE

Linguistic atmosphere is located in a specific time and place, with specific people, and is the key to intersubjectivity through language. Who controls the linguistic atmosphere? The linguistic atmosphere is where most power struggles occur, as is evident in the control exercised across our institutions like schools, courts and hospitals. Sometimes the only choice available is to withhold one's contribution from the linguistic atmosphere. Perhaps the linguistic atmosphere is the present time subconscious taking in and interpreting the intentional expressions which are part of the linguistic atmosphere.

Even animals have their own linguistic atmospheres tuned to the types of noises they can omit. Birds, dogs, humans, all sorts of animals have overlapping linguistic atmospheres, all of which one can tune into as the linguistic or iconic environment.

Society builds autonomous structures to control and manufacture and direct human movement. Courts, schools, mental hospitals, all have systems of reward and punishment for appropriate use, timing, and even the right to use language. By manipulating the linguistic atmosphere, the bearers of rights control the minds and thereby the actions of others around them.

Language is a sixth sense, a human sense, and the initial basis for the existence of the god-concept.

THE GOD-CONCEPT

The god-concept is the second most damaging concept in human history. How many people have committed murder for their god-concept? Every war is a holy war, a battle of ideals and human life. No single side of a war was not fought in the name of a god-concept. We would be much better off with a realistic god-concept, or none at all, which really amount to the same thing. How much money in the world has been spent in creating and perpetuating a god-concept, which, like the soul-concept, is simply a blatant fiction and a lie.

If you have to believe in something, believe in yourself. Replace your god-concept with your self-concept and you can't go wrong. Then read as many varied self-help books as issues arise, and you learn to be an active participant in control of your life.

Churches are an inherent means of control over the internal linguistic atmosphere. Get rid of the priests and religion loses its power. It remains a book, just another book.

You should have full power over your god-concept. You should make it in your ideal self-image. You should define for yourself what all-being means to you, what your self-determined role in the Universe is. You should figure out for yourself who you are, for the process is the journey, and to tell someone who they are is a corruption of their fundamental freedom to be themselves.

THE ABOLITION OF THE SOUL-CONCEPT

The soul-concept is probably the most destructive and offensive concept in human history, and it is a lie. Nobody has a soul, since such a thing has never existed, and it is a power game used to control the self-image that people have. The most sacred thing people can influence is their own identity, and taking that away from someone is spiritual murder.

There is no single part, not the brain, not the body, not the mind, that alone can be called the self. It is how the mind processes symbols of objects in the world and the words of other people, how the mind-brain-body system interacts with the Universe and with the cultural artifacts used by society that makes a person who they are. It is not merely the fact of subjective experience combined with a self-concept. These are just one side of the experiential continuum, mediated by the senses or otherwise how they may be.

Since the sense of the self as any one thing, and not as its true multiplicity of being, is nothing but an ignorant close-minded lie, the perpetuation of anything conscious by itself is downright offensive to the beauty of life. Science is but one method for obtaining knowledge about the Universe, but it is slow based on the fact that it is an inherently social method. But if the soul is part of the Universe, if it exists, then it is subject to the scientific process, or must be acknowledged as pure fiction, if no proof of non-physical existence can be shown to anybody and everybody.

The self-concept should be your primary concern. By knowing about yourself, you can know how to make and keep yourself happy. Your self-concept is sacred, and can be self-determined if you want it to be. The soul-concept retards this process of development. It denies your freedom to just be yourself.

PART B

CHAPTER 10:
SCIENCE OF REALITY

Reality is partly what you do with it and partly everything else that happens as also factual. By what you do with it, I mean freedom of will, or will-power and ability. Everything else that happens is at the other end of the intentional continuum, and is the subject of this essay.

Since reality includes what happens to you as well as what you do about it, we shall first look at the one end of the spectrum, the continuity of causation, leaving people out as a special topic to be handled in the next section on human freedom. For now, let's treat people as informational black holes travelling through the space-time continuum, or the black box problem in logic.

If the object side of experience is pointed at things, then the things are subject to the laws of the Universe, namely causation and continuity of parts through space and time. Every existent perceivable or imaginable thing has a volume and duration of existence. The being of the thing is the similarity of itself, in concept, to perception and memory. Imagined things have not yet been actualized, at least to your knowledge, for otherwise you would recognize them, though the fact that you can express recognition without prior experience poses a problem, though is one that can be studied by science. Though in the end it all comes down to experience, that ever changing constant that is present from just prior to birth until the last beat of the heart, the last breath, the final thought. Death is a very private moment for a conscious individual. It is the unreflectable moment.

Maybe consciousness is a cyclic process in the brain, repeating itself or moving forward or backwards through experience in memory, or tangent to memory but using the basic elements of experiential hardware, brain cells used in perception with connections that make up memory, and consciousness is a middle brain wave or cyclic pattern, with upper and lower limits, sleep at one end and shock at the other. Staying depressed or anxious all the time can lead to problems all their own, based on brain chemicals, of which it is the job of medicine to discover and provide cures. But the brain is incredibly flexible and has multiple layers of interpretable meaning or information, with reversible experience and world sensing moods that change without conscious intervention. They may alert us to danger, obliterate every other thing than the content of your adoration, or become tedious and unresting. Consciousness is a whole brain process and integrates all kinds of sensory input from many different types of nerve endings which becomes all the same type of nerve in the brain. But maybe that's not right. Maybe there are as many or more types of nerves in the brain itself as there are in the rest of the body. Maybe our sensory experience is based on more than just different forms of changing energy. Maybe it is the reversibility of experience backwards through the brain connections that makes reflection and consciousness possible. And maybe the connections themselves follow some sort of logic, or maybe that is the origin of random action.

The Universe is a whole other story. The fundamental laws that occur on Earth are the same throughout all space, time, energy and matter. That is why it is so important to find a reliable set of fundamental laws such as the speed of light, Plank's constant, gravity, electricity and magnetism, and the strong and weak nuclear forces. These are just some of the known ones. You could also throw in general and special relativity, if you wanted.

Science is slow and tedious work, but can be very rewarding socially and internally. Comprehension of a scientific concept can be obtained in mere moments, but some experiments need teams of scientists over several lifetimes to reach repeatable solutions. Anything that science has confirmed can in theory be observed by anyone, hence the repeatable and incremental approach to truth. Some hypotheses can be observed with multiple interpretations, leading to further hypotheses for experiments. Science in this sense becomes a self-fulfilling prophecy that perpetuates itself in cycles, which themselves can be studied by science. Science is an attitude with which you approach the Universe, both questioning and presuming, and is cumulative in its approach to truth, getting ever finer detail and certainty. Its primary role is to discover the fundamental laws of the Universe and its limits.

If nature is a fundamental law of the Universe, then different life forms, like bacteria, may exist on another planet in another solar system similar to ours. In fact, if life were a fundamental law of the Universe there probably is life somewhere, given the vast number of planets, comets, moons, and meteors in the Universe.

The fact of life existing elsewhere should not be nearly as exciting as the fact that life already in fact exists in the Universe, that is, here on Earth. The complexity of life forms on Earth is incredible, let alone the billions of species that have gone extinct since life began here on Earth. Maybe, given the evolution of the earth in its beginnings that were just about right for life to emerge naturally, as a consequence of initial conditions, randomness, the vast number of mere particles that make up the earth, and a lot of time, a lower energy order is bound to emerge in the form of self-replicating molecules. Life only needed to start once, the process that is, though it probably started and went extinct a number of times before the conditions were right for it to stick around. If so, we may be able to simulate the origin of life on computers to better understand evolution in order to control it.

What are the rules or regularities of the linguistic atmosphere? Are there ways that overlapping linguistic situations combine to make up the linguistic environment? Are there rules for the human linguistic atmosphere, and are these rules in some way based on consciousness?

If this is so, the so called objectivity of language is fundamentally based on subjective experience. Reading and writing language shapes the linguistic atmosphere in different ways than listening to and watching television. Conversation is again all together different, as different as the first, second, and third-person perspectives. Each opens us to a new world, a new layer of meaning and interpretation of the Universe.

The first, second, and third-person perspectives are by definition interpersonal. Each draws attention outward or inward, depending on the contextual situation. The first, second, and third-person perspectives can also be emphasized as different developmental stages. The final stage would be internalization of the linguistic atmosphere, problems of which may be the hearing of voices in your head, or in the world when alone, without the recognition that it is in fact your own voice internalized and controlled. When this control breaks down, the experience of living ghosts or encounters with the god-concept take place. In the medical community this is known as schizophrenia, and if symptoms persist, chemical intervention may be required.

In first-person perspective, you are engaged with your experience, such as reading these words right now. Following from experience, you are engaged with a world of objects, such as the markings on this page. But if you choose to disengage from the world for a bit, you are free to do that, but as you do that you engage the inherent factors of your mind, namely, imagination and memory through peripheral consciousness. You engage a concept and it takes hold of your attention throughout the duration of its process. Eventually you wake up and again engage the external world, acting on it as you will and desire. There is one dimension of control, inward applied outward through action, and outward inward through learning. Babies are born into a world perspective, then grow into their bodies and separate themselves from the world by learning control. This creates an inward-outward continuum that has pretty much crystallized by habit at some point during adulthood.

We are all aware of the first-person perspective, intimately and by reading this book. By reading this book, you have engaged with the second-person perspective. You took, and are in the process of taking on, the meaningful perspective of another person, even if only for arguments sake. In this way, you are engaging the linguistic atmosphere which inherently includes other people. Babies need to be an actively engaged participant in conversation when words are first learned. Without this mutual engagement and allowance for freely constructive syllables acting as words, which we now know are placeholders for multiple meanings, sometimes spontaneously, and require the context of conversation to be developed into autonomous language use. Part of the development is the ability to express one's free-will. Deprived of this opportunity to participate in the linguistic atmosphere, children may develop social problems later in life. Other people are inherent in language acquisition, use, and development, and often its purpose. Communication, whether visual, written, heard, or engaged in conversation, requires a minimum of two people, or the same person over time. Being an observer of a conversation, you engage the direction of attention of each person, in sequence, taking on the feelings of each person respectively. It is feelings that allow us to communicate, because without knowing where the other person is coming from, you cannot match your contribution to theirs, balancing perspectives. Eventually you can learn to apply the internalization of your own pattern of linguistic behavior and the expectations you have of encountering others, into a process that you can carry with you all day long, usually holding repeated fragments of a song or messages to yourself for later, or held to a book or movie or song or some other external cultural artifact. By playing devil's advocate for yourself, you can begin to take on other, multiple perspectives. This is where the moment of choice begins, when the consequences of any number of actions becomes apparent, at that moment, you must decide what to do next, even if it remains nothing. This is where the experience of figuring out your own self-chosen life purpose becomes highly useful. You can use that as a starting point and work backwards towards the present along multiple paths to help decide what to do next. Having this option available makes freedom possible. Without having memories and expectations as part of the present moment, expectations held in memory as the future present, we would be responding automatically to our senses of what is now around us.

But what if you are observing a conversation and the conversation becomes just about you, emotionally, while the context of the conversation, the words, which are capable of a multiplicity of meanings in the same and different contexts, are about something, anything, different and objective, impersonal, and not about you at all? If you choose to remain an objective observer, you must follow the words as spoken. The conversation remains about the state of the world. But what if you choose to associate with the secondary messages found in the choice of selected words, chosen intentionally or otherwise? If you could engage these underlying feelings, this power struggle, you could then choose your words carefully to direct the conversation in a more positive direction, by directing the object of the conversation, its content, to something new and exciting by expressing yourself carefully so as to negotiate the feelings of the two or more conversational participants. But when your name or reputation comes back to you from complete strangers, you have become a cultural icon of which your body becomes the artifact. If people approach you, your reputation precedes you, in which case reciprocate kindness.

Other people are not just other minds, but also other bodies that occupy the same Universe as your own. When touching, their body and yours occupy the same spatial point or surface of contact, perhaps even the same volume of space. Taken together, even without contact, multiple bodies make up a territory. Being Canadian, we take up all of Canada as our own. We own what we control, even if control is temporary or imagined. From childhood on, most of us control most of our bodies, or so we think. In fact, nature controls most of the details about how our bodies function, we just control the large muscle groups, some breathing, and some use of our brains, plus the timing of our digestive system. Beyond that, environmental control becomes more complex and we are forced to turn to the specialized skills, knowledge and ability of others, not to mention their willingness to help (for which money serves as a good motive). However, money should not replace enjoyment as the reasons for your actions. Enjoyment is a self-fulfilling prophecy and an end in itself.

Values and identity are essential to a sense of reality. Values shape the priority of tool use and the sequence of actions from the present into the future. Values may have a monetary equivalent or an emotional equivalent in the way they prioritize things and direct our attention. What is important to us gives us a sense of our own identity, as what we value. How we value things gives us a sense of ourselves as the source of value. Human beings give value to the world and invest meaning into things. What things mean to us gives us a sense of value to the world and invests meaning into things. What things mean to us gives us a sense of value to the world. What we mean to ourselves indicates the level of our self-esteem and self-respect. This is why I say, if you have to believe in something, if you have to have faith in something, have faith in yourself, believe in yourself.

Your self-concept is the most important concept as it is an awareness, or lack thereof, that most affects how you will approach your world, the feelings and intentions you have for things, which thereby simultaneously determines your intentional behavior towards things and other people.

How you gain self-knowledge is a process or journey through a world of possibilities. If your self-concept is true, then its knowledge is subject to the scientific process. This process can be done individually, for example keeping a journal (the most sacred book), or in a group, as in some counseling, or by others, such as doctors or teachers or in front of an audience.

How exactly is a self-concept formed? It has something to do with reflection, projection, and language development. Maybe it is the ability to actively move backward in time to understand cause-effect relations, then enacting the cause to bring about the desired effect. Maybe it is in entering this conceptual relation that builds a reflective feeling about oneself. Maybe recognition comes with the early forms of language acquisition, when others teach them how to control their bodies and thereby their mind's development in making grammatical linguistic utterances. Maybe the self-concept is a cultural artifact composed of a unique set of universal concepts that could apply to many others that exist. It is the body and the connections in the brain, the DNA usually, and identifying with one's own life that makes one's self unique, having one continuity of experience that only you have direct access to, to use in imagination which is also a part of your experience. Sometimes, though, your imagination gets out of your control, and takes over use of your body and mind. This is when you should seek help from trusted professionals and close friends. Keep working at it and eventually you can get your life back under control and take ownership of it. Slow, steady increases make up for unexpected temporary setbacks. And have faith in yourself that eventually you will be better. There's absolutely nothing wrong with always trying to improve yourself. That is how you can continue to grow. And when you reach a plateau in ability and interest, try something new. Always try new things if you think you might like them, it's called following your intuition and living spontaneously.

How can we tell what is real and what is not? One way is by asking other people, another way is based on the continuity of your senses. Since meaningful interpretations and intentions may occur spontaneously, as does objective perception following an attitude of observation as prior to intention, the act of doing something solidifies possibilities in a here-and-now actuality. As the body is under one's control, tool use also becomes under control, whereby the tool becomes an extension of one's body and being, and its successful use adds another ability to one's self-concept. Before coming back to the here-and-now, one is caught up in a timeless duration, where temporal expression occurs as a series of events leading to some final goal at a specific time. This is the case in sports, interpersonal events, pretty much anything you have to do or finish by a certain time. Even if you don't know how, you gain certainty by knowing the time. This is interesting because it is as though there is a singular objective time that is the time, and everybody's series of internally ordered events cannot change time's inevitability. But in interpersonal events, it is internal intentions that motivate how and when and for how long interpersonal interaction occurs. These events are successful based on a mutual understanding. The timing of sequential and simultaneous events helps.

So what isn't real? Obviously not every thing, being, or event is real, so how do we differentiate dreams and imagination from everyday normal life? Certainly in dreams, if you have a thought it automatically changes the world, whereas in waking life you are aware of the world surrounding your body, and you can withdraw from this world into imagination by overlapping perceptions by generating new ones using the same senses, and then return to perceiving the world around your body. In dreams there is no overlapping layer of imagination or thought, just a direct connection with your world. Lucid dreaming is like taking a step in a dream, it adds that intentional layer to the subjective side of the object-subject continuum of experience.

Although not everything happens for a reason, a reason can be attributed to any event through interpretation, but this does not mean that the interpretation is actually true.

If we cannot differentiate in experience the causes of our experience, we automatically assume it is external, as part of something out there in the world. When the source is internal to your body, you take possession of it. But when it is internal to your mind, or ambiguous, you may hold uncertainty as to its being. Causes are not reasons, though there may be a multiplicity of causes preceding an event, they hold together as a singularity in the event. There may also be a multiplicity of reasons for an event which may not necessarily be causes or effects, but remain intentions.

It is in imagination that the god-concept can be said to exist. Therefore, try this thought experiment. Just imagine for a moment what the world would be like in the absence of any god-concept. Really imagine the whole of the Universe, with human beings having the special place of culture and imagination inherent in their evolved bodies, without any interference of the god-concept. Because, really, there is no place for a god-concept in a Science of Reality.

Reality comes from the integration of a number of processes; social processes, cultural processes, habit, one's prior experience, one's physical history or spatiotemporal continuity, your self-concept, the processing of here and now experience, the laws of nature and the laws of the Universe. Therefore, reality is not singular, though the object of attention may be, but may be viewed as the integration of these processes. Some people take one of these processes and hold it up as the measure of reality, but any of these viewpoints or worldviews can be offered as a basis of comparison for any other. Each is a unique worldview, but it is how they all come together that makes up the Science of Reality.

With computer technology blurring the boundaries between special effects and human acting, it's getting harder to believe anything on television. The internet is becoming a better source of information, but is becoming overloaded with mere information without the critical restraint and censorship of television stations. We are constantly filling our time without a plan to guide it. Capitalist investment processes have resulted in more debt than there is money. Money has only exchange value, for labour or products.

How do you create a god-concept? First, you need a physical symbol, like the Automat. Then you attribute properties or characteristics to the object that you would like to have for yourself. In this way you can draw on your icon for the internal support or power or any other characteristic during the course of the day. Simply by touching your object you can transform those properties into yourself when needed or lacking. The final step is to give your object a name, as a symbol of the deity you also have thereby created, by giving it, too, a name. This is how a god-concept is born, and it is within your individual power to create a god-concept, and it is empowering to do so. By reflecting on the properties of your god-concept in this way, you also gain direct self-knowledge, by creating your own antithesis as your ideal self-image while keeping you grounded in the world.

The Automat is the symbolic person, one arrow pointing down to the body, another arrow pointing outwards, into the world, at things or other people. These two arrows connect at the top, forming a new arrow pointing to reflected consciousness or the self. The self is the ground of all being, other people and the Universe the ground of all existence, your own body included and ever-present.

I have labeled my god-concept Lukrishna, for no specific reason. It consists of an ordinary drinking straw, folded in on itself at the ends after making three folds in the straw. It becomes a three dimensional triangle, and each of its properties has a meaning. First, it can be replicated for free, even made from trash on the ground. Second, it takes human action to make, making it a cultural artifact. Third, the straw itself is like the body's skin, making a boundary between itself and the world. The body itself has an inside volume and an outside, like the self-concept within a body without organs, simply a self. Looking through the triangle is actively engaging consciousness, blocking out the rest of the world in order to focus on another object or person, thereby contextualizing objective experience. The three sides of the triangle represent feelings, thoughts, and actions, or meaning as portrayed through emotions, the mind, and the body. It is self enclosed and autonomous, being an object, but it is one way of portraying yourself to yourself, taking a one dimensional straw; realized as a two dimensional surface enclosing an eternal circle; the third dimension comes with the act of folding the straw in on itself, symbolically adding dimensions to its existence. I make one and place my faith in its ability to act as a placebo for the self-fulfilling prophecy of ability. By believing in Lukrishna, I invest my faith in myself and can fearlessly look into the unknown, knowing I have my full history of experience to automatically act accordingly with the anticipation of new knowledge.

Your consciousness is of objects in the environment, but the source of this experience is in a body which has its own environment. The world is in us only so far as we are aware of the world. The way we move from object or property to object or property is through shifts in attention. Language mediates attention. What we hear we become conscious of. What I think about when I see something is mediated internally by language and objectification. By believing in yourself, you set up a self-fulfilling prophecy about your excellence, on which habits of excellence can be based and modeled for others. You do this by shifting your awareness to what is peripheral to your conscious attention onto something positive about the situation, thereby controlling your moods, a process that can be mediated by internalized language, or the linguistic atmosphere.

CHAPTER 11:
HUMAN FREEDOM

What is freedom? What is normal? Is freedom normal, and if not, would we still want to be normal? Normal is a social phenomenon where we are all cultural contributors.

The ability to move, breathe, and experience can certainly constrain one's freedom, as well as contribute to it in controlled ways.

How can you measure and quantify, how can you add numbers to the linguistic atmosphere to bring it within the realm of science? You can measure the tempo, rhythm, and amplitude of the language use of those around you, the frequency of key words, or the way concepts overlap across conversations. The mood of a room is one quality of the linguistic atmosphere.

True freedom involves manipulating the linguistic atmosphere at will, for others, without feelings of shame or guilt. The drive for normality deprives you of making original contributions to culture.

Let's begin with freedom as the characteristic of getting to do what you want, and analyze that perspective. How are habits designed to enforce and impair freedom? Surely healthy habits create more free time while unhealthy habits leave no time for oneself.

Memory and imagination use the same hardware in the brain, though each function may be dominant more in one hemisphere than the other, for recollection or projection. This difference determines our internal sense of time.

Hemisphere dominance takes place automatically, but the real issue for free-will takes place between amplifying and inhibiting neurons. Active neurons take one part of consciousness and make it our awareness. When one doesn't want to think about something anymore, they actively inhibit it to keep it out of their conscious awareness by keeping it in their peripheral consciousness and focusing on something else. This is where the ambiguity of meaning in language can express disjointed thoughts through causal processes from the body that communicate to others across the linguistic atmosphere. Freedom develops over the lifespan.

A belief is not a thing, it's a process, a way of perceiving the world. There should be a dual epistemology, the causality of the Universe with the freedom of human possibilities. These two sides should be separated as distinct but overlapping realms, freedom and the Universe.

Everything that exists is real. But reality is more than the totality of all that exists. Reality also includes human freedom and everything this produces. The contents of imagination can be said not to exist, but imagination itself is real, so in a sense the contents of imagination can direct the behavior of your body, which is physical, and through action and will-power the contents of your imagination can enter into the causal continuum of the Universe.

So what is not real? Let's use the example of the god-concept. Here is something that exists only in human imagination. How is this concept put together? First, names are socially transmitted, crystallizing a perception. But a perception of what? Cultural artifacts and the being of the self. Songs, pictures, movies, books, stories, myths, icons, metaphors. Did you know that in Canada as of the time of this publication, that it is illegal to change your given name to the word 'God'. Hopefully, in the future, this will change. Until then, the identity behind the god-concept is the self.

Reality can be studied both personally, on the basis of one's own experience, and scientifically on the basis of shared experience. Since reality incorporates both sides of experience, the interpreted side and the intended side, which are both sides of the same simultaneous experience, reality can be studied objectively and subjectively and still be talking about the same thing. And in talking about reality, we necessarily enter into an inter-social atmosphere, a linguistic atmosphere, influenced by other human freedoms, and is a purely human phenomenon. The linguistic atmosphere is where culture lives in real time, spread over space. By listening to the linguistic atmosphere, people enliven culture and add meaning and value to the present moment even if only an interpreted meaning. When you talk to someone, you intend to communicate something. But your intended meaning may not be interpreted how you intended it. Even in miscommunication something meaningful occurs, and an interpersonal situation takes place.

What is a self, a whole self with well-being? These, actually, are two different things, an actual self reading these words, and an ideal conception of a self in general, as presented in this book.

Every self is the source of all being, all meaning in the world, and even the world itself. Not the Earth or the physical Universe, but the everyday world, the world in which one lives. But where does meaning come from? Mostly from applying the scientific attitude by reducing meaning from one's direct experience. Also from other people. Other people add meaning to one's direct experience.

So how does one direct one's own experience to develop oneself, and make for oneself an adequate self-concept or ego?

Once again, we can turn to the wholly imaginary god-concept to understand the ego concept, of which the self-concept becomes aware of itself. How can one begin to objectify oneself from oneself, if one identifies wholly with one's subjective experience? I believe people are more than just the inside of their experience. Every living person has a living body, whether they identify with it or not. One is one's body, in the sense of existing. And one is also one's sense of experience, the totality of meaning given to things, even those meanings held in peripheral consciousness and never consciously recognized but that makes up the world. And each person, on the basis of existence alone, began by other people, grows with other people, are enculturated and learn language and habits from other people, even role model them.

The really interesting thing about people, on the basis of their existence, is that they can enter into mutual causal relations with one another, initially making contact through the linguistic atmosphere, and can take it one step further, initiating causal relations with oneself over time.

Other than physical force, of which only the government can authorize in the form of police, and those violent crimes such as rape, murder, and assault, and those affectionate gestures such as a handshake, a hug, or making love, most causal interaction takes place at the emotional level through participation in the linguistic atmosphere. Communication changes beliefs.

What is free speech? The fact that a person can state the truth about the purely imaginary god-concept as a concept and not an existent being, created in order to force the dominant power's authority on people, this, my friends, is freedom of speech.

How one interprets oneself and one's god-concept in light of these revelations is a wholly interpretive act. My role is merely to guide you along the process of self-discovery.

You have the ability to plan for your future. By making intentions now, and since habits build on habits, you can actively bring your past into your future right now.

How does free will work? First, you must set up a conscious intention or goal. Then you plan with the resources available. Then out of many possible courses of action you choose one. Then you act, investing meaning into the future turn of events, by establishing a past foundation for further action in the present. Finally, once the goal is achieved, you recognize your intention in the project's fulfillment, and move on to do something else. You can be working on multiple intended goals at the same time, even combining actions to accomplish many things simultaneously. Part of acting on free-will is by keeping your goal in peripheral consciousness by focusing your attention on doing the immediate steps to reach your goal. Engaging free-will is the basis for the self-fulfilling prophesy.

How does free-will affect the choices of others? This is the realm of inter-subjectivity or shared experience. Have you ever heard of the song in the head theory? It is basically the linguistic atmosphere internalized into an autonomous presence. Meditation works because it turns off the linguistic atmosphere from thoughts, leading to a more natural and relaxed state.

One part of ourselves that I have left out of discussion is that part objectified and held in another person's brain, their experience of us. Through others we are judged, labeled, objectified, with very little control over our externally perceived self image experienced by others. Not only our actual self and ego is expressed at all times, there is also other people's experiences of your self. So your self actually occupies matter, space, and time, but also our field of experience and our social existence, our reputation. Ignoring or trying to over-control these aspects of your self can result in mental illness.

How do reality and truth occupy human freedom, and what impact does free-will have in these realms of measurement? For this may be where numbers and experimentation can be applied to the field of reality.

How can I prove to myself that I exist? One way is by reading this book. In order for these words to have meaning, they must be understood and interpreted as meaning something. By maintaining interest, I can demonstrate to myself that these words are a meaningful intention by the author to make a point, and even if you don't get the themes, you still know you exist by fulfilling the meaning of these sentences and by understanding them. This means someone must be reading meaningfully, otherwise these would remain meaningless marks on a page somewhere. Another way is by initiating and enacting a motive of free-will. Human beings give meaning and value to the Universe, which serves the basis that human freedom is an inalienable right.

Money is good for two things; collecting and spending. Things have a price, and this is where money comes into exchange for goods, services or labour, and tax. Goods and labour have use value, and it is in their use that they add value to the world and to your life.

One way of applying numbers to human freedom is to treat everybody the same and start counting the degrees of freedom in a community or even over all of humanity. But everybody is not the same and uses their free-will differently. So this method of applying numbers to freedom doesn't work. Some people are freer than others. Should we really move to equality and disvaluing individual strengths and weaknesses? I think not. A good use of numbers in human freedom is to count a habitual action in order to objectify the habit and change or control it on the basis of that self-knowledge. Another use of numbers is to make a pros and cons list for a given decision, choice, or prelude to action. By making an exhaustive list of both pros and cons, an objective decision can be made on the basis of subjective data. There are many useful ways of applying numbers to human freedom, which makes this a scientifically investigatable realm, namely, the Science of Reality.

The null hypothesis comes in handy when doing controlled experiments with oneself, with the outcome for action remaining the same and uninfluenced by the action. The self-fulfilling prophesy is free-will in action. It uses peripheral consciousness to bring into attention the recognition of the intention in the fulfillment.

By making a wish, by filling your heart with desire for something or someone, you create for yourself a powerful image for the future. Then, after time, you forget and move on towards other things, other people. But one day, you realized that all the things you had wanted at one moment in your life now surround you. It is because the original wish was a real moment in your life, and never left your mind. It remained accessible for consciousness at any moment, but stays out of awareness until it enters perception and activates the initiatory imaginary event. This is not to say that every imaginary event will at some future point come into existence, but rather that some do. And that is where the self actively enters the causal process of the Universe from imagination to reality and back into memory. Meaning structures allow for the past to materialize in the present, and the present thereby becoming future held in the past.

You have the freedom to enter causally and intentionally in the process, the temporal course of your life. But sometimes you need something physical to reflect your memory and maintain perception of your intuition in physical form, thereby objectifying the process of the self-fulfilling prophecy in action.

This physical object can take the form of pills, Lukrishna, a picture, a rabbit's foot, really anything in which you can invest personal meaning, meaning just for you, which includes to some degree everything you use. Other people can invest the belief in you that certain objects, people dead or alive, or simply beliefs themselves, can change your life in some way that you desire. Through the placebo effect the self-fulfilling prophecy can flow naturally. But it is not all positive. Sometimes the mind can cause pain, dizziness, strong emotional or allergic reactions, and so forth. In some cases the mind can actually cure the body and itself by staying positive in affection and intention. Staying positive in intent can create well being and actually overcome psychosomatic illness, with or without a placebo, and can be maintained by positive, self-affirming habits.

Once you have a concept in mind, you can use it as a surface into which or from which you can choose where next to direct your attention. This can take the form of looking deeper into a perception, looking at the world surrounding the conceptualization, or in any of a number of other directions.

The most important concept is the concept of the self. The self is the source of all freedom and all value. Every self has a body, but not every body has a self. Often the self is associated with the brain, but you need not identify with your nervous system any more than the chemical composition of your blood. You need both to live, but you are far more. You are both the interpreter and producer of your own reality. Your self is at the center of your experience. You can also create yourself. You have that power, that ability. It is all about where you direct your attention in the moment.

What are the limits of the self? The being of being is a linguistic problem, whereas the point of existence is a stable space-time-matter-energy problem. Some things, such as the god-concept, can have being without existing, namely as imaginary conceptions that become a habit through which experience is filtered. I believe in myself, and so should you.

CHAPTER 12:
PERIPHERAL
CONSCIOUSNESS AND THE
LINGUISTIC ATMOSPHERE

Where does freedom come from? Certainly not from the god-concept, but from where? Being human. Humans have evolved to be free, and from there have been enslaving one another ever since. It is not the awareness of one's own inevitable death that leads to freedom, but from a willingness to life one's own life despite the inevitability of uncertain death and by controlling one's own body and the linguistic atmosphere for others through one's bodily actions. And since the brain is part of one's body, it is just as much the common architecture of the human brain that allows for control of its memory for consciousness which it can then communicate. Imagination is what makes humans free. Perhaps this is why artists, actors and musicians are so well paid and respected. They create and provide for others a fantasy world that others can relate to through imagination.

Religion tries to steal your very experience from you, to take ownership of your very human being, and to subject it and you to their very whim and control. I say, take back control of your life, take ownership of your very personal being, your self, and live the dream of freedom. Accept your freedom for what it is, and take responsibility for your life. Cast off the invisible shackles of religious, political and social control and create your own future. This and this alone is your human right, namely, the right to be free. So be free, enjoy life, take some drugs and explore the limits of your experience. You only live once, don't give your life away to someone else that only has the interests of their group in mind. Instead, be selfish, indulge, and realize that other people are a necessary part of your life, even if only through culture or memory, and that they are basically doing the same thing as you, so respect their inherent freedom to choose and act, and at the same time respect yourself and your right to live. Remember, your self, your well-being, should be your first priority, and that learning and adaptation are basically the same thing.

Peripheral consciousness is that part of the world you were just conscious of and about which you are going to be conscious of. It is temporally located as the antithesis of the present and spatially as what is not here. It is the world surrounding the object of consciousness and contains all you are aware of or capable of becoming aware of at a given moment. Peripheral consciousness includes memory and imagination as well as the perceivable world. Consciousness blocks things out to hold a single awareness of its object. All that gets negated or blocked out goes into peripheral consciousness. The linguistic atmosphere makes extended use of peripheral consciousness, if nothing more than to hold the whole meaning of a sentence in the mind for its understanding.

Whereas your peripheral consciousness is everything you are aware of without it becoming the focus of your attention, the linguistic atmosphere is the overlay of the physical environment with cultural meaning. The interaction of a person's linguistic atmosphere with that of another person makes up an iconic environment, wherein intersubjective interaction takes place. An iconic environment can extend even to the edges of the Universe and is the whole of cultural meanings extended onto the physical Universe. It is the whole symbolic layer of understanding in real time, not held by cultural artifacts but changing in time to suit the needs of specific people interacting in a social manner. Every gesture, every interpretable act or thing, constitutes an iconic environment wherein a linguistic atmosphere can take place.

Freedom in the linguistic atmosphere is entailed in the right to freedom of speech. Anyone can manipulate the linguistic atmosphere, and it is social conditioning that defines the right to speak for any individual within that society.

When you're shy, or socially phobic, you become extra aware of the linguistic atmosphere, even preoccupied by it, paranoid and frozen the in moment that could be an opportunity to exercise your fundamental freedom as a conscious human being. Other people are just as important as me and I am just as important as them.

We each have a right to exist, to influence the linguistic atmosphere and direct our own growth. The Science of Reality hopes to show how to live through your right to exist.

CHAPTER 13:
THE UNIVERSE, THE
SELF-CONCEPT, AND
INTERSUBJECTIVITY

SYNTHESIZED REALITY

Let's travel through reality in a little mental experiment. An inward journey if you will. Let's leave this place and venture out into reality, to see what we can find.

We start by travelling out from the self-concept, towards other people or things. Towards all things we aim at, we begin with our self and our surroundings. Being a body, we occupy the same physical Universe, and can influence the linguistic atmosphere for any other person, directly or indirectly, at any particular moment, as demonstrated in the numerous text messages and video conferencing now available on the internet.

Let's begin by directing our attention outward. The outer world is characterized by causal continuity. Space-time and matter and energy constitute all things.

We start with the self and end at the self.

Perception. You perceive your self as perceiving the perceiver. But this is at the opposite pole of experience than the objective world. Unlike objects of imagination, there is always some doubt or error concerning the certainty and magnitude of the thing's existence. However, the outer world, the physical Universe, is all that exists. Therefore doubt and uncertainty is just a necessary approximation to the complexity of the situation.

Is there such a thing as non-physical energy? Definitely not. Unlike dogmatic faith, scientific inquiry gradually progresses towards the truth in finer and finer detail. This process reaches its absolute limit when technology can look no deeper and this does not mean that all knowledge in incorrect, but rather is in the process of being corrected by reducing possibilities.

The brain. Some neuron signals prevent other certain neurons from sending a signal, and with others enhance or provide the initiatory push for a new signal in the receiving neurons. The brain has most of the nerve cells in the human body, but not all of them. Being a self is no more than being your toes as it is being the focal point of your eye's retina. Your being extends out from your body by valuing certain things over others.

Part of your self includes the tools you use in everyday life. This constitutes your territory, including your body. Inherent in your muscles are automatic memories that perform habitual actions, but you can consciously intervene to change them, even if only temporarily.

Extending your self outside of your body is one way of entering into groups of other people. Other people have other bodies, and thereby a natural territory they can call their own. By sharing tools and projecting your aims towards others, many people can contribute to the same project, even if that project is social construction. We can engineer our culture by providing society with the necessities of life and something they can do to improve themselves, and thereby society itself, something like lifelong learning and completely free and fully accessible education.

Even though you can never become your tools fully, you can claim right to shared ownership over them, as you can about your part in culture and shared society. Mutual co-existence defines shared reality.

How do you come to know about the Universe? You can either have ideas communicated to you by other people directly in dialogue or from cultural artifacts such as books, songs, video games, television, and so on. Once you have obtained a concept you can apply it to your perception to see if it fits with the object of your awareness and your expectations. If not, then you can either move that concept to your peripheral consciousness and try another one, or shift your attention to another object in your environment. Knowledge occurs when the recognition of the concept and the object coincide. When this occurs it is possible to label the experience whereby the experience, or its object, may enter into the linguistic atmosphere.

How do you develop the intention to learn? By questioning your belief structure based on experience. Where does being come from? From human beings.

Where does the self come from? From being human. One answer can suffice for every question, but it doesn't get us any closer to the truth. In fact, truth is a process, a search for gaining knowledge and understanding how things happen.

The process of growth is a process of self-discovery. It never ends, until your death. Death is the end possibility of all experience and action. Death is the unreflectable experience. Unless someone else saves your life. This complicates all philosophies not based on care for one another. Sometimes you can reflect on the moment just preceding your physical death. This moment could change the rest of your life, or it could be just another moment. I guess this could be said for any moment, any experience.

Dreams just happen to you. Unlike your goals, you have no control over your dreams. In this sense, dreams are more free than your conscious waking life, and dreams make manifest to yourself the fact that you are not even in total control of yourself. Your conscious, waking life may not always have total control over its body or its linguistic atmosphere, but your self-concept in dreams is completely out of control, mainly because your body is partially paralyzed. This unreflectability in dreams is, in part, the processing of the day's events for the next day's events, which can extend indefinitely in time and space, and even your body. To say that dreams are intentional may be to misinterpret the meaning of meaning. Since space and time of dreams does not actually exist, there is only here and now in dreams but no concrete physical self, aside from the living, breathing body of the dreamer. The meaning of dreams is an interpretation, but the dream itself is a fulfillment, an unintended experience. Therefore, in interpreting intentions into dreams that may have meaning, even though dreams are the effect of random spinal cord stimulation, leading to interpretation as more processing of random signals leads to order, the dreaming life and waking life both contribute to the continuity of experience. Not all experience is intentional.

The linguistic atmosphere has no material history and that is how it is physically transcendent while also being physically dependent.

A certain amount of relativity is necessary to understand one another, but dogmatic skepticism does not foster effective communication.

Good and bad are interpretations of actions, not people. There is no such thing as a good person or a bad person. There is only self-interested people and there is nothing wrong with that.

Self-interest is in everybody's best interest. By improving ourselves, we directly improve society by being a part of that society. By being a role model you share your world-view such that others can copy it and thereby improve themselves. Self-interest has individual's and society's best interest at stake.

You can think about what you're saying, but thinking takes time and so you are limited in time by what you could possibly say. Therefore, to save time you habituate ways of talking, and this opens your conscious attention to making a relevant contribution between habitual responses. Most processing of the linguistic atmosphere happens automatically, and it takes practice to actively listen.

Much of the brain is active in the background of your experience, and by focusing your conscious attention to something, you use only a small percentage more of your brain activity. This lends incredible support to the theory of peripheral consciousness, wherein what presents itself to consciousness gets processed in an understandable order. For the brain provides what you are to become conscious of next.

This connects the temporal succession of the body with the atemporal processing of the journey of the mind through past, present, and future, fixing consciousness in the here and now through perception or the focusing of attention. And the outer world is grounded in space and time.

When we look outside of ourselves we are taking in information. We see colours and shapes, but before we see those, we see things. We perceive that we are seeing something, and are therefore conscious of something. We are not forming things internally and projecting them onto the world from the third-person perspective. We are immersed in a three-dimensional, changing world and add layers of interpretations onto those objects that contact our experience. By reflecting, we are making present the learned structures of our brain and bringing past meaning into the future through the present. We find around us a given world, a world that is the same as itself except that it includes us, free beings, human beings.

We are all culture producers, even as babies. Every meaningful gesture we make can be represented to someone, even if the interpreter is the same person as the producer. When we express ourselves to others, we leave our identity open to interpretation in the social sense.

Even if we let our minds wander into black holes and superstring theory, quantum observer effects, or the curving and warping of space-time, we still get no closer to knowing who we are.

If beliefs manifest behaviours, then believing in yourself will automatically manifest your desires.

Chapter 14:
The Science of Human Autonomy

Freedom and self:

So where does freedom come from? It is the awareness of one's own life by controlling one's own body and the linguistic atmosphere for others through one's bodily actions. And since the brain is part of one's body, it is just as much the common architecture of the human brain, provided by human DNA, which allows for control of its memory for a consciousness that it can then communicate. Imagination is what makes humans free. Perhaps this is why artists, actors and musicians create and provide for others a fantasy world that others can relate to through imagination and relating the experience to their self-concept.

What is a self, and how is it free?

Let's begin with nothing. Absolute nothingness at the beginning. Not even words or concepts. Just empty your mind.

Now imagine a dot, just a dot. From the perspective of this dot, it sees only nothing. It has no sense of space or time because it has no frame of reference. It is even unaware of its own existence since it has no body parts from which to infer results of intentional action. This imaginary dot exists only in imagination, as it would have nothing to think about.

Now, imagine a second dot. This changes everything. As a second dot, consciousness is now possible for the first dot, as it now has something to be conscious of. This second dot becomes the whole world for the first dot. Now from that second dot, the first dot can direct its conscious awareness away from that dot and onto other things, like the thought of that dot. This is where thinking begins, which can produce thinking about thinking, and inevitably a self-concept. Others are the basis of the self-concept and we need a world in order to think.

Thought is totally free. Consciously directed imagination is the source of human freedom, and laying out possibilities for future actions and situations.

Now, let's jump into another world, a world that exists after we die and before we were born, and that necessarily includes our own body and the bodies of other people. We wouldn't exist without two people coming together to reproduce. Now we are more than a mere dot, we have a full body with which to influence each other, enter into the linguistic atmosphere, and have a causal influence on the universe.

Let's expand now to three dots in imagination. Now there is the possibility of language and the linguistic atmosphere. There is the possibility of central and peripheral consciousness.

Three free points of view defines an intersubjective group. Two people can discuss the third, who may withhold making a contribution, with coded cover stories to express their emotional reaction to another about another. This, and this alone, is the universal third-person perspective, and can occur between anyone and at least a pair of strangers, with at least one person to bear witness to the cover story.

THE SCIENCE OF HUMAN AUTONOMY

Now, let's direct our attention inward for a minute. The inner world is defined by freedom. Experience freely associates, and meaning is defined by interpretation and instant recognition of ideas.

If we start with the self and end with the self, where do we find our selves? We find our self when we look inward, a detachment from perception to reflection and anticipation. How we are feeling has a lot to do with the types of memories we are capable of recalling with clarity.

Introspection is a tricky bugger, since every time you look at it, it vanishes. It is something that just happens in the brain. The brain can detect other existence more easily than its own consciousness.

Where does your body end and your self begin? Are we limited in action by beliefs or morals about what would be good or bad for our self?

How do we identify ourselves to ourselves? One way is by use of our personal name. Another is by the universal symbol of identity, 'I' am. Which should we prefer, the general or the particular? Or are these roles reversed from our own perspective?

Self-esteem is very important. It is both based on your feelings about yourself and your confidence in your ability. Shyness is like a prison for yourself, where you are encaged by your own body, from which you are effortfully trying to escape. Self-esteem helps with shyness because you no longer depend on the reactions of others to give your life meaning.

What do you consider to be of greater truth, what you were told by someone, or something you can see and feel for yourself? Both can be genuine sources of knowledge and genuine sources of error.

When you go inside, you withdraw from the world. You can be comforted with the certainty in the contents of your mind, even if those contents are irrelevant to what is going on around you. Uncertainty is a law of nature, but not necessarily of the mind.

The inner side of experience reveals the true self no more than does the outer side of experience. They are both just directions for attention to survey the self from both sides.

Experience just happens, we cannot control every act of experience simply because other people add elements of freedom to the causal structure of the Universe through adding layers of meaning to a simple object. Each layer adds a fresh perspective on an object, increasing the meaning given to it. It is almost like in perception when we intend to perceive something and are just waiting for the fulfillment of our expectations. Not everything nor everyone should be controlled anyways, even if this is technologically possible.

Creativity is at the core of being human since it exercises the imagination and develops new meanings for things, new ways of connecting with the world around us. Creativity is something everybody is capable of, which means that everybody has at least one tool with which to solve their problems. Teamwork thrives in the attitude of creativity. Limits are overthrown, boundaries are pushed, and the status quo need no longer survive. Down with normality, up with creativity.

Normality has certain problems of its own. Normality is especially important in the linguistic atmosphere, where you say only what is expected of you. Why try to be normal when you could just be yourself, upon which the very concept of normality is based.

Learning is also very important. Self-directed enculturation requires in you the responsibility to shape yourself into anything you want to be, and one way of going about this is by learning from yourself what you like and dislike. Learning and self-directed enculturation are matters of taste, not ethics.

Morality poses one of the biggest problems for freedom. That one should live according to an ideal is wholly unnatural. Freedom is also freedom from externally imposed standards of behavior. But rules and freedom are not mutually exclusive so long as one chooses those rules for him or herself.

Being a self is like being a body without organs, just an integrated whole. But problems occur if this whole breaks down or is replaced with an alternative identity.

A personality is composed of all those habits you choose not to do anything about as well as those habits you are unaware of. In order to change a habit, it must first occupy your conscious awareness. You cannot intentionally change a habit or your personality without becoming aware of that trait first, even if that trait is only held in peripheral consciousness.

It is through conversation that we build our identity in others, as well as theirs to our self. Every conversation is a compromise in order for it to succeed. Since everyone is trying to save face, even mistakes are allowed into the linguistic atmosphere, so long as they are immediately corrected.

When you go inside, you push your surroundings into the background of peripheral consciousness. You may put up a defensive shell and not let anything get through, or you may simply let your mind wander, outwards into the possibilities of the world. You may drift back and forth, between the words of another while off in an imaginary world. As part of a group of three, two people may relay messages while the third either listens, or carries on a communication pattern like a circle that intermittently reverses. This is the linguistic atmosphere at its finest. Each person, taking turns, fills the void of background noise with an intentional will to communicate, including some and excluding others by making an intention mutually manifest. Language extends to cover the whole body, and every physical manifestation can communicate these actions, accompanying such actions or not. But interpretation and intention do not always initially match up. This is where communication skills, not logical or analytical skills, would come in handy. Being able to express an opinion, belief, or intention accurately and adequately takes practice and patience, but with open-minded persistence, you can relay a rational reason, however distorted it may be to your initial self-representation.

Where can you go if you need to escape a situation and you cannot go anywhere? You take a vacation in your head, dissociating your conscious mind from your body. You can drink until you black out. You can smoke salvia. You can remember you are free to change your interpretation of the event, and free to choose how much meaning and emotion to put into the present situation.

In any case, you can choose to escape yourself, you can make plans for the future to defer action for the moment, or you can take control of your body and how you choose to believe in your self in order to express yourself adequately.

You go where you believe you should go. You go there for some reason that has value for you, and in going there you bring your attention from the periphery to the center of your awareness.

Emotional reasoning goes as follows, and is a logical error, though while undergoing emotional reasoning the thought patterns seem logical enough. I am me in the sense of being aware of an underlying continuity of experience that is my life. I am self-aware. Being self-aware, I understand that I have emotional needs and other feelings of which I can become aware at any time, in other words, my feelings occupy my peripheral consciousness and I may focus on them at any point. When I am trying to solve a problem, emotional or otherwise, I often look for what is bothering me in the environment around me. We do not always have control over our emotions.

Therefore, if I am undergoing emotional strain, I believe that there must have been a cause for my feelings, and I begin to search my environment for the source of that cause. If I am feeling upset or troubled, I look for what is troubling me. I may be unaware that the source of my despair has nothing to do with what is going on around me but may be sourced in drugs or hormone changes. Still, I look around to see if I can find an object to get mad at, to hold accountable for my change in emotional pattern. If I find nothing to be the source of my emotional response, I may blame others for what they have just said, or I may blame the things around me for not working properly. None of this, of course, has anything to do with intentional changes in my emotional state, merely having a body will induce feelings of tiredness or hunger or thirst. Any emotion may be produced by the body, and usually in response to awareness of some aspect of the environment, but this is not always the reason for the emotional change. This is the anatomy of emotional reasoning, and I hope it is clear how this is a logical error, since in trying to solve a problem, an emotional problem, you appeal to the cause-effect structure of the Universe hoping to find the source of the problem in order to find an adequate solution to the initial problem, or at least its cause in the environment, when the cause was actually internal to the person's body.

CHAPTER 15:
CONCLUSION

In conclusion, let us discuss world domination. What is meant by 'world' domination, or for that matter, a 'world' to be dominated? But before I expand on world liberation, there is an important distinction to make between being and existence when talking about a world. Being and existence do not refer to the same logical realms. As a whole, existence refers to the physical Universe while being refers to all that is, in other words, a person's subjective world of experience. But both realms meet in the particular moments of perception and learning. Being refers to possibilities, existence to perceivable things in the sense that they are verifiable beings. Existent things may have a multiplicity of beings or interpretations, and this is no less so than in the linguistic atmosphere. Peripheral consciousness makes use of possibilities, while existent things or concepts focus one's attention, thereby collapsing possibilities into one concrete being. World domination can refer to world liberation, by becoming as free as possible by working with the elements of your world and worldview.

I am my body. I am my mind. I am other people for other people. I am a human being being human. I am not ideal, but I am real. Perfection breeds contempt for normality. Normality is an ideal, not a mathematical average. Normality is a concept, just like a god-concept and a self-concept. Being free means living outside of concepts, acting freely with your body. The self-fulfilling prophesy makes sure that your body brings out what is intended by your mind. Believing in yourself ensures you have the confidence to support your self-fulfilling prophesies.

This mysterious free-self is an ideal concept, but can be brought about by changing your perception of your self-concept into that of a totally free being. This liberates your self-concept from the control of others and empowers you to become whatever you wanted to be. The god-concept and the soul-concept retard this progress towards self-liberation.

Have faith in yourself, believe in yourself, and you can never do wrong by your own standards. Believing in your future self enables you to get through tough times, and believing that you can solve any problem allows you to begin to do so. Even if you don't know the answer now, believe that in your future you will be able to figure it out. This is what belief in your self means. Belief in your self builds confidence and self-esteem.

You are all that you do as well as all you believe and feel. If you believe in the truth, you never stop questioning it, because if the truth is out there it will answer each and every valid question that the mind can come up with.

But even if the answer is false, this does not mean that the question was properly framed, taking the self, others, and the Universe as the basis of all knowledge. You are free to believe anything you like, but your belief may be wrong when tested against the measure of reality as a whole integrated system.

Now let's return to the idea of world domination. Does world in this sense refer to the realm of experience or the physical Universe? Since it makes no sense to dominate all of nature across the whole Universe, world domination must mean control over one's own experience. But experience includes other people and other freedoms. Does world domination mean taking possession of other people's experience as your own, controlling and manipulating their actions, thereby eliminating their freedom for the sake of your own? If this is true, it actually reduces freedom in the Universe despite increasing your personal range of control. Would not world liberation be a more practical goal? I propose it would.

Why is it so important to be creative, unique, and autonomist, about being free and independent? It is because you have a single, unique body, even as twins, and it is your responsibility to care for yourself, identify your wishes, and self-direct the course of your life in order to take care of your body. Life entails growth and adaptation, and human life entails learning. Blind acceptance of a norm in order to be normal is the most direct barrier to personal growth.

And when organized religion is a part of the norm, you forfeit the only right you really have as a free being, the right to live your life and define your experience to yourself. Nothing can take your life experience away from you, but some people try through various techniques of brainwashing, such as organized religion. Unfortunately, the brainwashed do not recognize the process, since they habituate the beliefs of others, and never get that objective view of the big picture. Rituals, traditions, unconscious habits, these things hold us back while providing the foundation for the future. By becoming more aware of the processes in which you are engaged, you can change the future by bringing your awareness from the past to the present. By questioning and acting in novel and new ways, you rupture the equilibrium of the status-quo, a necessary rupture for social change to occur. The world could tolerate a little more insanity, by which I mean creative disregard for social conventions.

How shall we go about world liberation? World in this sense designates all human beings, making this a very political question. But, there is a solution and I need your help. I cannot divulge all of the steps involved in attaining this goal, in part, because this has never been done before. But I can lay out a process, goal, or future plan that may help. And it directly involves our children. Children's rights have been as ignored as prisoner's rights, which is another avenue of freedom to be explored. I have opened with many questions, some of which will be answered in future works, some because an open mind can never close. This book is not an ending, but the beginning of a process. So let's now look at one way that world liberation can come about.

The biggest challenge and obstacle to world liberation is governments. They put up barriers to keep their population inside, more than anything else. The second limitation is blind acceptance of social norms, including organized religion. Finally, there is the barrier of ignorance, invisible yet dominating. This last one I wish to address the most, because this is where the most headway can be achieved. Liberation through education. A world education system that indoctrinates freedom.

Every person can be better in some way. And by improving yourself, you do the most possible to improve society, automatically by being a part of a society. Helping others to improve can occur by improving yourself and by simply being yourself as a role model for others. You can be an other for one another. And improvement comes from self-directed learning.

So what we need is a free education system where people can learn what they want when they want, thereby accelerating their natural learning speed, not held back by the external expectations of what you should know by when, and how much you are worth being based on a number, such as a grade or income. You should instead be measured by what you can do with the concepts you have learned. The present education system is inefficient and ineffective, and works about as well as the prison system, in terms of self-development. These systems need to change. Even prisoners have the right to self-development, otherwise why hold them in prison for any duration of time, if they are not expected to be better people for being put through the process. Jail just makes smarter criminals, since they have the chance to reflect on what they did wrong, why they got caught, and how they can do it better next time so that they can get away with it from now on. Rather, prison should be more like schools. And schools should no longer imprison children until a certain age and are then free them to escape the education system after high school. Schools are not day care centers so that children's parents can earn money.

Children need more rights, due to the natural state of their dependency for food and shelter. Children are a vulnerable group of people. We were all children, we never grow up, we just continue to learn or at some point just stop growing. And schools are definitely not necessary for people to be able to learn. Schools should directly and indirectly teach children, adults, prisoners, anyone how to use their own mind and respond to the feelings of having a set of inherited emotions.

What we need is a politics of mutual freedom, and a mode of co-operation on a global scale.

With all of this said, I cannot do all of this alone. Let us start together a non-profit corporation for free, universal, and accessible education. This is just a starting point for social change on a global scale. Every person alive has the right to think any thought, to learn any concept, to develop their skills in any way they desire. Education is a right, not a privilege. In this way we can provide the means by which every person has the potential to be equal to every other person, regardless of gender, age, nationality, ethnic origin, historical period, personal life experience, general attitude, or any other trait by which people define themselves. None of this matters when you define yourself, and others, as fundamentally free beings, as human beings. Every person has the right to life regardless of their past actions, not every egg or sperm or zygote or fetus, but every person who has a working heart, brain, and lungs, or adequate substitute when these fail.

As a side note, children enter the linguistic atmosphere from their first breath onwards. Through crying, having not yet developed a symbolic language, babies are able to communicate, to indicate their needs and affections. It is the responsibility of every parent to make sure these physical and emotional needs are met until a child is capable of independent living. It is at this point that children should enter the economic sphere, not out of the necessity to fulfill their own needs, as that is the role of an adult and parent, but to expose them initially to the economic and political practices that will serve the foundation for their future self-dependence. Children should have the right to vote, as soon as they learn to sight-read or determine words, such as a party or candidate name. Society as a whole would benefit because it would allow children to practice having an influence on the world and become autonomous cultural producers.

I hope this book was as fun to read as it was to write, and I am looking forward to revising this book to reach a wider audience, based on your feedback. If you have any suggestions, criticisms, complaints, or appraisals of this book, really any opinion at all concerning the subject matter of this book, please do not hesitate to write and send an e-mail, or multiple e-mails, to the e-mail address at the back of this book, or visit the website, a perpetual work in progress that will eventually host the world's first extensive, free education system. But to build this system into existence, I need your help. Please take just enough time to respond to this book as you need. Then, if you enjoyed it, give this book to someone else you know and actively pass on the message. Together, we can do this, we can make this happen. And if you really liked this book, buy multiple copies for your family and friends. Pass it on.

Appendix:
The Automat

AUTOMAT:

The Symbol of Choice, the Essence of Human Freedom
The automat is the symbol in the title of the title page.

It represents the moment of choice, emanating from the self at the top, and going out into the world. There are many dichotomies that this division can represent, but the important thing is that any situation can be negated by reversing the direction of the situation of choice and going back into the self, the arrow created by traveling backwards from the world into the self, a choice present in any choice. The automat is the ultimate symbol of the Autonomy Foundation, and represents all we do.

Following this lead, it can be said that every person is a combination of thoughts, feelings, and actions, which is represented by the body of the Lukerishna. The Lukerishna is the idol of the god of man as himself. In order to create a Lukerishna, representing the body of man in his totality, one must follow these instructions:

First, take an ordinary drinking straw. Put three bends in it. Then fold the shortest end length wise and insert it into the other end of the straw. This creates an isosceles triangle, representing the three dimensions of mankind with its three sides; cognition, emotion, and behaviour. The act of inserting the two ends represents the act of creating a new person, by which mankind propagates. The straw itself represents the skin of the body, mankind's largest organ and the barrier between oneself and the world. Inside the straw is the void, the body without organs, the need to be filled. By looking through the straw, we exercise consciousness, a limited and objectifying perspective on the world. By looking around the straw, one is in touch with one's world. By taking an everyday object and investing it with this meaning, we proclaim our divine ability to give meaning to ourselves and our world.

There is also a way of symbolizing human interaction with one's own body. By connecting both hands at the thumb and index fingers, with all other fingers extended, one can represent the four aspects of the human being; thoughts, feelings, sensation, and intuition. These correspond to the four outstretched fingers, with the thumb representing negation, a uniquely human characteristic. With palms faced out, and thumbs and index fingers connected, we can make contact with each other through our bodies, occupying a single point in space for a limited duration of time, representing mutuality within our finite existence. Through the triangle formed, we can view each other consciously as complete human beings. If we wish to objectify an object in the world, we need only extend our index and middle fingers only, connecting our thumbs representing the possibility of negation, to reduce our viewed object the mere sensation and cognition. This is only done to things in the world, as they lack the necessary subjectivity that defines human being. By curling our thumb over our four fingers, we negate humanity through the fist. This should be avoided at all costs, since such actions make conscious understanding impossible and thereby deny the principle of mutuality.

Freedom, Truth, Mutuality
These are the principles of the Autonomy Foundation.

www.autonomyfoundation.com

e-mail to:
freedom@autonomyfoundation.com